bubblefacts...

KNIGHTS AND CASTLES

Miles Kelly

PUBLISHING

First published in 2005 by
Miles Kelly Publishing Ltd
Bardfield Centre, Great Bardfield, Essex, CM7 4SL

Copyright © Miles Kelly Publishing Ltd 2005

2 4 6 8 10 9 7 5 3 1

Publishing Director:
Anne Marshall

Senior Editor:
Belinda Gallagher

Editorial Assistant:
Hannah Todd

Designer:
Louisa Leitao

Cartoons:
Mark Davis

Production:
Estela Boulton

ISBN 1-84236-522-3

Printed in China

British Library Cataloguing-in-Publication Data
A catalogue record for this book is available from the British Library

Indexer: Jane Parker

www.mileskelly.net
info@mileskelly.net

Contents

 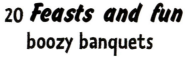

In the beginning...
castle capers!

A castle was both a home and a fortress in the Middle Ages. It provided shelter for a king or a lord and his family, and allowed him to defend his lands. Castles were also places where soldiers were stationed, wrong-doers were imprisoned, courts settled disputes, weapons were made and banquets and tournaments were held.

Wooden castles were not very strong and burnt down easily, so stone castles were built from the 1100s.

The first castles were mostly built from wood on top of a hill called a motte. On the motte stood a wooden tower, or keep. This was the central part of the castle and the easiest area to defend.

The builders of early wooden castles covered the walls with wet leather to protect them from fire.

CAN'T... QUITE... LIFT!

LIGHTWEIGHT!

COME ON LADS, TIME FOR A TEA BREAK!

Stone castles were stronger and gave better protection from attack, fire and the weather.

Building a castle

hard graft

The best place to build a castle was on top of a hill. A hilltop position gave good views over the surrounding countryside and made it harder for an enemy to launch a surprise attack. Sometimes a castle was built on the banks of a river or lake and its water was used to create a moat.

WHERE'S MY HAMMER...?

CATCH! HA HA!

VERY FUNNY... LAUGH-A-MINUTE ROUND HERE.

COME ON. PUT SOME WELLY INTO IT!

BZZZ!

SQUEAK!

SCRAPE!

Building a castle involved hundreds of workers, from labourers to stone masons and carpenters.

The planning and design of the castle were managed by a mason. Supplies were brought in by river.

The lord of the castle lived in the keep, the safest part of the castle. Its thick walls were well-guarded.

Castle capers

who's who?

A castle was the home of an important and powerful person, such as a king, a lord or a knight. The lord of the castle controlled the castle itself, as well as the lands and people around it. The lady of the castle was in charge of the day-to-day running of things. She controlled the kitchens and gave the servants their orders for feasts and banquets.

Servants lived and worked inside the castle, cooking, cleaning and serving food to the lord and his family.

There was no bathroom for the servants. They had to take a dip in the local river to wash – and get rid of any fleas and lice!

The constable was in charge of defending the castle. He trained his soldiers to guard the castle properly and he organized a rota of guards and watchmen. When the lord was away, the constable was in charge of the entire castle.

I WANT MY DINNER AND I WANT IT **NOW!**

TEMPER TEMPER!

WHAT'S HE **BANG**ING ON ABOUT?

BANG!

Inside the castle walls were workshops where important tools and weapons were made and repaired.

King of the castle

castle VIPs

In medieval times, the king or queen was the most important person in the country. The king gave land to his barons and other noblemen. In return, they supplied the king with soldiers, horses and weapons to fight wars. This system of giving away land in return for services was known as feudalism.

The Church was powerful in the Middle Ages, and it grew rich from charging peasants to live on its land.

Barons were the most powerful noblemen – they supplied the king with men who would fight.

At the bottom of the feudal system were peasants. Everything they owned belonged to the local lord.

Good knight!

how to be one

It took about 14 years of training to become a knight. The son of a noble joined a lord's household at the age of seven. There he learned how to ride, to shoot a bow and arrow and how to behave in front of nobles. He then became a squire and learned how to fight with a sword.

LOVE ME, LOVE MY HORSE!

ARISE, SIR KNIGHT!

WHERE'S YOUR FIGHTING SPIRIT! WHOOOO!

Men were knighted in a dubbing ceremony. The night before the ceremony was spent praying in church.

A knight who behaved badly was disgraced and punished. He may have behaved in a cowardly way on the battlefield, cheated in a tournament or treated another knight badly.

A French knight sent love poems to the Countess of Tripoli, even though he had never met her. When he finally saw her he fell into her arms and died.

Knights followed a code of chivalry. This involved being brave in battle and treating the enemy fairly.

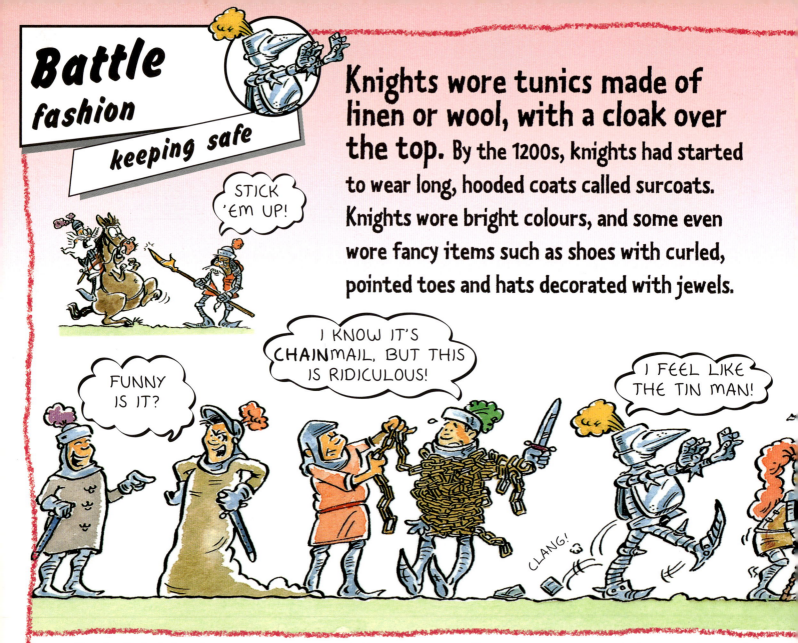

Battle fashion

keeping safe

Knights wore tunics made of linen or wool, with a cloak over the top. By the 1200s, knights had started to wear long, hooded coats called surcoats. Knights wore bright colours, and some even wore fancy items such as shoes with curled, pointed toes and hats decorated with jewels.

Gradually knights began to wear more and more armour. They even wore metal gloves and shoes!

Soldiers called 'retrievers' had to run into the middle of the battle and collect all the spare arrows!

Early knights wore a type of armour called chainmail. It was made of thousands of tiny iron rings joined together. A piece of chainmail looked a bit like knitting, except it was made of metal, not wool. A knight also wore a padded jacket under his chainmail to make sure he wasn't cut by his own armour!

England and France were at war between 1337 and 1453. This long dispute was called the Hundred Years War.

Famous knights

knightly capers

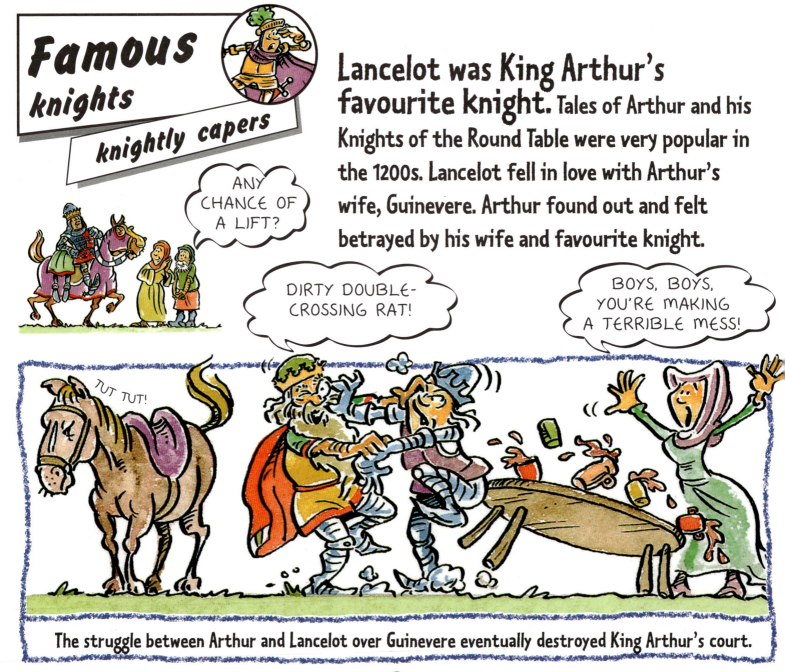

ANY CHANCE OF A LIFT?

Lancelot was King Arthur's favourite knight. Tales of Arthur and his Knights of the Round Table were very popular in the 1200s. Lancelot fell in love with Arthur's wife, Guinevere. Arthur found out and felt betrayed by his wife and favourite knight.

DIRTY DOUBLE-CROSSING RAT!

BOYS, BOYS, YOU'RE MAKING A TERRIBLE MESS!

TUT TUT!

The struggle between Arthur and Lancelot over Guinevere eventually destroyed King Arthur's court.

The book *Don Quixote* tells the story of an old man who dreamed about past deeds of bravery and chivalry. It was written in the 1500s by Spaniard Miguel de Cervantes. After reading about the knights of old, Don Quixote dressed in armour and set off on horseback to become famous.

During his travels, Don Quixote mistook flocks of farmyard animals for enemy armies!

LAZY GOOD-FOR-NOTHING!

ZZZZZZZ

WHAT DID YOU CALL ME?

Don Quixote dreamed of being a knight. Spanish knight El Cid fought against the Moors of North Africa.

Castles had no central heating and no running water. Wool hangings and tapestries on the walls helped to keep the rooms warm. Roaring fires burned in huge fireplaces.

The centre of activity was the great hall. This was where banquets and important meetings were held. In the kitchens, meat sizzled on spits in front of the fire. The bedrooms were cold and draughty. Fresh reeds covered the floors as there were no carpets.

Almost all castles had a well within their walls. This was an essential water source in a siege.

Castle key

1. Gatehouse – the tower and gates that guard the entrance to a castle.

2. Great hall – the big business room that was used for banquets and feasts.

3. Portcullis – a heavy metal fence that sealed off the castle gateway.

4. Tower – a tall building from which enemies could be seen.

5. Machicolations – small chutes from which missiles could be dropped on the enemy.

6. Battlements – walkways that were defended by stone blocks.

7. Arrow loops – narrow slits in the walls through which archers could fire arrows.

Every castle had a cold, dark, slimy dungeon for holding prisoners, who were locked in smelly cells.

Feasts and fun
boozy banquets

The great hall was the centre of castle life. The lord and his family ate their meals here and carried out their daily business. Colourful banners, coats-of-arms and shiny pieces of armour hung from the walls. The hall was sometimes turned into a courtroom to try law-breakers.

ROWDY LOT!

YUMMY!

GLUG

FILL ME UP, WENCH

IS THIS ORGANIC?

NO, IT'S CHICKEN!

Jesters, jugglers and sometimes even a dancing bear performed for the diners between courses.

can you believe it?

The Turks fought with gold pieces in their mouths to stop the crusader knights from stealing it.

The lord, his family and important guests sat at the high table on a platform called a dais. From their raised position they could look down over the rest of the diners. The most important guests such as priests and noblemen sat next to the lord.

Huge amounts of exotic-looking food were served at banquets. Roast meats were very popular.

Songs...
poems
...and love!

Medieval minstrels sang songs and recited poetry about love and bravery. These songs and poems showed knights as faithful, loving and religious men. A true knight fought for justice and fairness for everyone. In real life, knights did not always live up to this ideal picture.

Minstrels sang their songs to the accompaniment of sweet-sounding music from a lute or harp.

A style of romantic behaviour called courtly love was popular among knights. It was a kind of false love carried out by following strict rules. Courtly love stated that a knight had to fall in love with a woman of equal or higher rank – and ideally she should be married to someone else!

A knight would offer to perform brave and heroic acts at tournaments for the woman he loved.

SCRIBBLE!

WRITER'S BLOCK... AGAIN

PSST! WANT SOME GOSSIP?

I'VE BEEN DUMPED! THE HUMILIATION... I'LL KILL HIM!

Troubadours were poet musicians who wrote about love. A knight would write secret letters to his love.

Knights and dragons

fiery fables

The legend of St George tells how a brave knight killed a fierce dragon. The dragon was terrorizing the people of Lydia (part of modern Turkey). The king of Lydia even offered his daughter to the dragon if it promised to leave them alone.

LEG IT!

OOH! YOU'VE SINGED MY BEARD!

FEELING HOT ARE WE? YOU'LL SOON BE A MOLTEN MESS!

George killed the dragon and the people of Lydia became Christians. St George is the patron saint of England

A crusader knight would share his tent with his beloved horse - it must have been a bit of a squeeze!

King Arthur had many castle homes but his favourite was Camelot. Historians think that Camelot was really an English castle called Tintagel. No one really knows who the real Arthur was but he may have been a Celtic warrior who lived 1400 years ago.

MERLIN, IT'S NOT AS EASY AS IT LOOKS...

MATE, THAT SWORD IS STUCK.

CALL YOURSELF A KNIGHT! WIMP!

POOR BOY!

Legend says that King Arthur became king after pulling a magic sword, called Excalibur, from a stone.

Practice for battle

play fights

In a tournament, knights divided into two sides and fought each other as if in a real battle. Tournaments were good practice for the real thing – war. The idea for these mock battles, called tourneys, probably started in France in the 12th century.

Jousting knights charged with a long pole called a lance. Each tried to knock his opponent off his horse.

Jousting was introduced because so many knights were being killed or wounded during tournaments. Jousting knights were protected by armour and their lances were not sharp.

Some knights cheated in jousts by wearing special armour that was fixed onto the horse's saddle!

SORRY IF THIS HURTS...

ME TOO, SHALL WE GO HOME?

ROUND TWO. DING DING!

JINGLE JANGLE!

WIMPS!

Sometimes knights would carry on fighting on the ground with their swords, but this was dangerous.

Castle
under siege
chaaaaarge!

An attacking enemy had to break through a castle's defences to get inside its walls. One way was to break down the castle gates with battering rams. Attackers and defenders also used siege engines to hurl boulders at each other.

HELP!

SHOW 'EM WHAT YOU'RE MADE OF!

CAN'T QUITE GET THE HANG...

CHAAARGE!

Giant catapults were used to fire stones or burning pieces of wood at the castle.

The ropes used to wind up siege catapults were made from plaits of human hair!

A siege engine called a trebuchet had a long wooden arm with a heavy weight at one end and a sling at the other. A big stone was placed in the sling, and as the weight dropped, the stone was hurled towards the castle walls, sometimes travelling as far as 300 metres.

WHOOSH!

PUUSH!

WE ARE!

YOU COULD TRY KNOCKING!

Soldiers charged with huge, heavy battering rams to smash down castle gates.

Castle defences
keeping safe

When enemies were spotted approaching a castle, its defenders pulled up the castle drawbridge. They also lowered an iron grate, called a portcullis, to form an extra barrier behind the drawbridge.

Defenders poured boiling water onto the heads of the enemy as they tried to climb the castle walls.

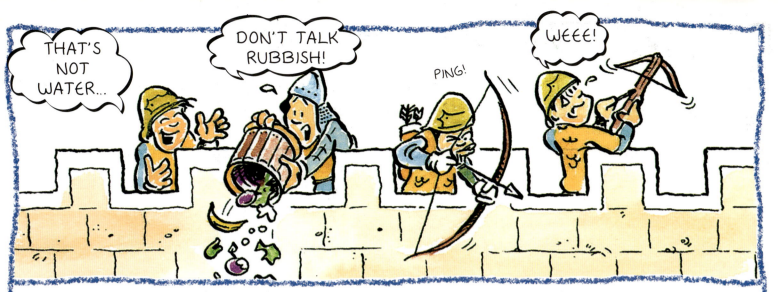

The castle archers fired their arrows through gaps in the battlements and slits in the castle walls.

In the night a group from inside the castle would sometimes surprise the attackers outside.

Index